Little Pebble™

Habitats

All About
Oceans

by Christina Mia Gardeski

CAPSTONE PRESS
a capstone imprint

Little Pebble is published by Capstone Press,
1710 Roe Crest Drive, North Mankato, Minnesota 56003
www.mycapstone.com

Library of Congress Cataloging-in-Publication Data
Names: Gardeski, Christina Mia.
Title: All about oceans / by Christina Mia Gardeski.
Description: North Mankato, Minnesota : Capstone Press, [2018] | Series:
   Little pebble. Habitats | Audience: Ages 4-8. | Audience: K to grade 3. |
   Includes bibliographical references and index.
Identifiers: LCCN 2016058057| ISBN 9781515776444 (library binding) |
   ISBN 9781515776505 (pbk.) | ISBN 9781515776802 (ebook (pdf))
Subjects: LCSH: Marine animals—Habitat—Juvenile literature. |
   Marine habitats—Juvenile literature. | Marine ecology—Juvenile literature. |
   Ocean—Juvenile literature.
Classification: LCC QL122.2 .G348 2018 | DDC 577.7—dc23
LC record available at https://lccn.loc.gov/2016058057

Editorial Credits
Kristen Mohn, editor; Juliette Peters, designer; Wanda Winch, media researcher;
Steve Walker, production specialist

Photo Credits
Minden Pictures: Hiroya Minakuchi, 17; Shutterstock: Bokasana, starfish design, wave design, CO Leong, 19, David Litman, 15, Kajonsak Tui, 9, KGrif, 13, Kjeld Friis, 7, mashe, 11, Soren Egeberg Photography, 21, Tanya Puntti, 5, Willyam Bradberry, cover, 1

Table of Contents

What Is an Ocean?

An ocean is a big body of salt water. Plants and animals live in oceans.

Their homes are called habitats.

Most homes are in water.

Some are on shore.

The Shore

Waves roll in.

Crabs hide in the sand.

Birds hunt.

ghost crab

Waves roll out.
Sea stars hold
on to rocks.

The Open Ocean

The sun warms the open ocean.

Kelp grows.

Fish live in the kelp.

kelp

Seals eat the fish.

Sharks hunt.

leopard shark

The Deep Sea

The deep sea is cold

and dark.

Big whales dive here.

sperm whale

It is hard to see in the dark.

Some animals grow big eyes.

Others glow!

jellyfish

The waves roll in and out.

Life is on the move in the ocean.

Glossary

crab—a sea animal with a wide, flat shell and two front claws

deep sea—the bottom of the ocean where it is cold and dark

habitat—the home of a plant or animal

kelp—a big, brown plant that grows in the ocean

open ocean—the top of the ocean far from land

sea star—a sea animal that has five arms and is shaped like a star

shore—the part of the ocean where the water ends and the land begins

Read More

Coss, Lauren. *Life in Oceans.* Life in Water Biomes. Mankato, Minn.: The Child's World, 2014.

Gibbs, Maddie. *Sea Stars.* Fun Fish. New York: PowerKids Press, 2014.

Leake, Diyan. *Oceans and Seas.* Water, Water Everywhere! Chicago: Capstone Heinemann Library, 2015.

Internet Sites

FactHound offers a safe, fun way to find Internet sites related to this book. All of the sites on FactHound have been researched by our staff.

Here's all you do:
Visit *www.facthound.com*
Type in this code: 9781515776444

Check out projects, games and lots more at
www.capstonekids.com

Index